I0428820

U.S. ENVIRONMENTAL PROTECTION AGENCY
OFFICE OF INSPECTOR GENERAL

Catalyst for Improving the Environment

Evaluation Report

Changes in Conditions at Wildcat Landfill Superfund Site in Delaware Call for Increased EPA Oversight

Report No. 10-P-0055

January 26, 2010

Report Contributors: Carolyn Copper
                                                         Patrick Milligan
                                                         Denise Rice
                                                         Martha Chang
                                                         Kathryn Hess

Abbreviations

DNREC   Department of Natural Resources and Environmental Control (Delaware)
EPA   U.S. Environmental Protection Agency
mg/L   milligrams per liter
MW   Monitoring Well
NPL   National Priorities List
OIG   Office of Inspector General
PCBs   Polychlorinated biphenyls
PRP   Potentially Responsible Party
ROD   Record of Decision
RPM   Remedial Project Manager
Site   Wildcat Landfill Superfund Site
SVOCs   Semi-volatile Organic Compounds
SW   Surface Water
TPH   Total Petroleum Hydrocarbons
ug/L   micrograms per liter
VOCs   Volatile Organic Compounds

Cover photo: The remediated Wildcat Superfund Landfill Site near Dover, Delaware.
                    (EPA OIG photo)

At a Glance

Catalyst for Improving the Environment

Why We Did This Review

The Office of Inspector General (OIG) is testing long-term monitoring results at Superfund sites the U.S. Environmental Protection Agency (EPA) has deleted from the National Priorities List. The Wildcat Landfill Superfund Site, located near Dover, Delaware (within EPA Region 3), is one of eight sites being reviewed. In April 2008, the OIG obtained groundwater and surface water samples from the Site and conducted a site inspection.

Background

Wildcat Landfill was added to the Superfund National Priorities List in 1983 and was deleted from the list in 2003. The Site was contaminated from disposal of paint sludge and municipal, industrial, and latex waste. In 2005, the Site was sold to Kent County, Delaware (Site owner), which plans to reuse the Site for public recreation purposes.

For further information, contact our Office of Congressional, Public Affairs and Management at (202) 566-2391.

To view the full report, click on the following link:
www.epa.gov/oig/reports/2010/20100126-10-P-0055.pdf

Changes in Conditions at Wildcat Landfill Superfund Site in Delaware Call for Increased EPA Oversight

What We Found

Our inspection of the Wildcat Landfill Superfund Site, combined with the current owner's plans for the Site, demonstrate that more sampling and EPA oversight are needed to ensure that the Site remains safe for humans and the environment based on planned future use. Our independent sampling results were generally consistent with Region 3's historical results. However, surface waters at the Site have a sheen that resembles petroleum. The clean-up remedy does not address petroleum contamination and Region 3 had not tested for petroleum during its sampling events, but agreed to test for it in September 2009. In December 2009, the Region reported that it had detected petroleum at levels below public health standards and it will continue to monitor petroleum levels at the Site.

OIG's results also disclosed several instances where aluminum, iron, and selenium exceeded ecological protection standards. Further, Region 3's historical samples were not always analyzed according to the required standard, which can prevent detection of contamination that exceeds standards. Region 3 corrected this error in a September 2009 sampling event. It also reported from its September 2009 sampling event that levels of aluminum and selenium were within ecological protection standards, but iron was not.

The Site has not been cleaned up to standards that allow for unrestricted public access. However, the Site's owner plans to create a greenway and to construct a bike path on the landfill, which would open part of the Site to unrestricted access. A local small business owner who purchased an acre of the Site has also inquired about building a storage facility on that acre. Region 3's oversight of the Site reuse plans has been informal and undocumented. The Region is currently aware of the Site owner's plans and agreed to formally document discussions with the Site owner and review reuse plans as they become available.

What We Recommend

We recommend that Region 3 modify its sampling and analysis approach to ensure proper testing of relevant contaminants, address contamination that exceeds ecological or human safety standards, and improve oversight of Site reuse plans. Region 3 agreed with OIG recommendations and has initiated or completed some actions.

UNITED STATES ENVIRONMENTAL PROTECTION AGENCY
WASHINGTON, D.C. 20460

January 26, 2010

MEMORANDUM

SUBJECT: Changes in Conditions at Wildcat Landfill Superfund Site
in Delaware Call for Increased EPA Oversight
Report No. 10-P-0055

FROM: Wade T. Najjum
Assistant Inspector General
Office of Program Evaluation

TO: Shawn M. Garvin
Region   dministrator

This is our report on the subject evaluation conducted by the Office of Inspector General (OIG) of the U.S. Environmental Protection Agency (EPA). This report contains the findings from our sampling at the Wildcat Landfill Superfund Site and corrective actions the OIG recommends. EPA Region 3 concurred with and provided comments on the recommendations of the draft report. This report represents the opinion of the OIG and does not necessarily represent the final EPA position. Final determinations on matters in this report will be made by EPA managers in accordance with established resolution procedures.

The estimated cost of this report – calculated by multiplying the project's staff days by the applicable daily full cost billing rates in effect at the time, then adding in the contractor costs – is $285,382.

Action Required

In accordance with EPA Manual 2750, you are required to provide a written response to this report within 90 calendar days. You should include a corrective action plan for agreed upon actions, including milestone dates. We have no objections to the further release of this report to the public. This report will be available at http://www.epa.gov/oig.

If you or your staff have any questions regarding this report, please contact Carolyn Copper, Director for Program Evaluation, Hazardous Waste Issues, at (202) 566-0829 or copper.carolyn@epa.gov; or Patrick Milligan, Project Manager, at (215) 814-2326 or milligan.patrick@epa.gov.

Table of Contents

Chapters

Appendices

Chapter 1
Introduction

Purpose

The Office of Inspector General (OIG) of the U.S. Environmental Protection Agency (EPA) is evaluating long-term monitoring at Superfund sites deleted from the National Priorities List (NPL). This is being done to ensure EPA has valid and reliable data on the conditions of these sites. The Wildcat Landfill Superfund Site near Dover, Delaware, is one of eight sites being reviewed. We collected groundwater and surface water samples and conducted a site inspection. We compared our results to past results reported by EPA Region 3.

Background

The Wildcat Landfill Superfund Site is located 2.5 miles southeast of Dover in Kent County, Delaware. The 44-acre Site is bordered to the north and east by the St. Jones River and its associated wetlands and to the south and west by residential and commercial development. The Site was operated as a permitted sanitary landfill between 1962 and 1973, accepting both municipal and industrial wastes. According to Region 3, industrial wastes suspected to have been disposed include latex waste and paint sludge. Region 3 indicated that the landfill owners routinely violated operating and other permits issued by regulating agencies during the landfill's 11 years of operation.

The Site was placed on the Superfund NPL in 1983. In 1988, EPA issued two Records of Decision (RODs) that described the clean-up goals and actions to be conducted – one ROD for each operational unit. Remedial actions included establishing haul roads throughout the Site, covering and re-vegetating barren/exposed areas on the landfill, draining and stabilizing an existing pond, stabilizing and capping contaminated soils onsite, removing drums, and establishing a wetland replacement pond known as the Wetland Mitigation Area.

The Potentially Responsible Parties (PRPs) completed construction of the two operable units in 1992. In 1992, groundwater monitoring was initiated to evaluate the effectiveness of the Site clean-up. EPA deleted the Site from the NPL in 2003, which signified clean-up goals were achieved through remedial action. In 2005, nearly all of the Site was sold to Kent County, Delaware; a small business owns about an acre of the 44-acre site.

Noteworthy Achievements

The selected remedial action for this Site included:

- removing and disposing of both hazardous and non-hazardous waste;
- grading the Site, installing a soil cover, and re-vegetating on-site direct contact risk areas;
- replacing two wells adjacent to the site;
- implementing institutional controls, including well and land use restrictions; and
- monitoring groundwater.

Documentation indicated the Remedial Project Manager (RPM) visits the site at least annually. The RPM inspects the site, looks for changes in land use on and around the site, and ensures there are sufficient sample data on which to make a protectiveness determination. Since it purchased the landfill in 2005, a Kent County representative stated that the County has removed large quantities of domestic waste and trash, and placed an earthen cap over a 12-acre area of the site.

Scope and Methodology

We conducted our work from February 2008 to September 2009 in accordance with generally accepted government auditing standards. Those standards require that we plan and perform the evaluation to obtain sufficient, appropriate evidence to provide a reasonable basis for our findings and conclusions based on our evaluation objectives. We believe that the evidence obtained provides a reasonable basis for our findings and conclusions based on our evaluation objectives.

We interviewed the Region 3 RPM and the Project Manager for the State of Delaware Department of Natural Resources and Environmental Control (DNREC). We also interviewed the Kent County Director of Parks Division, a representative for the Site's current owner, Kent County. We reviewed relevant guidance and Site documents such as the ROD, Five-Year Reviews, operation and maintenance reports, and institutional control documents.

We acquired a qualified contractor to take groundwater and surface water samples, and conduct a site inspection at the Site in April 2008. The OIG's contractor collected samples from three groundwater monitoring wells (MW-1B, MW-17, and MW-4) and two surface water locations (SW-01 and SW-02). See Figure 1-1.

Figure 1-1: Wildcat Landfill Map

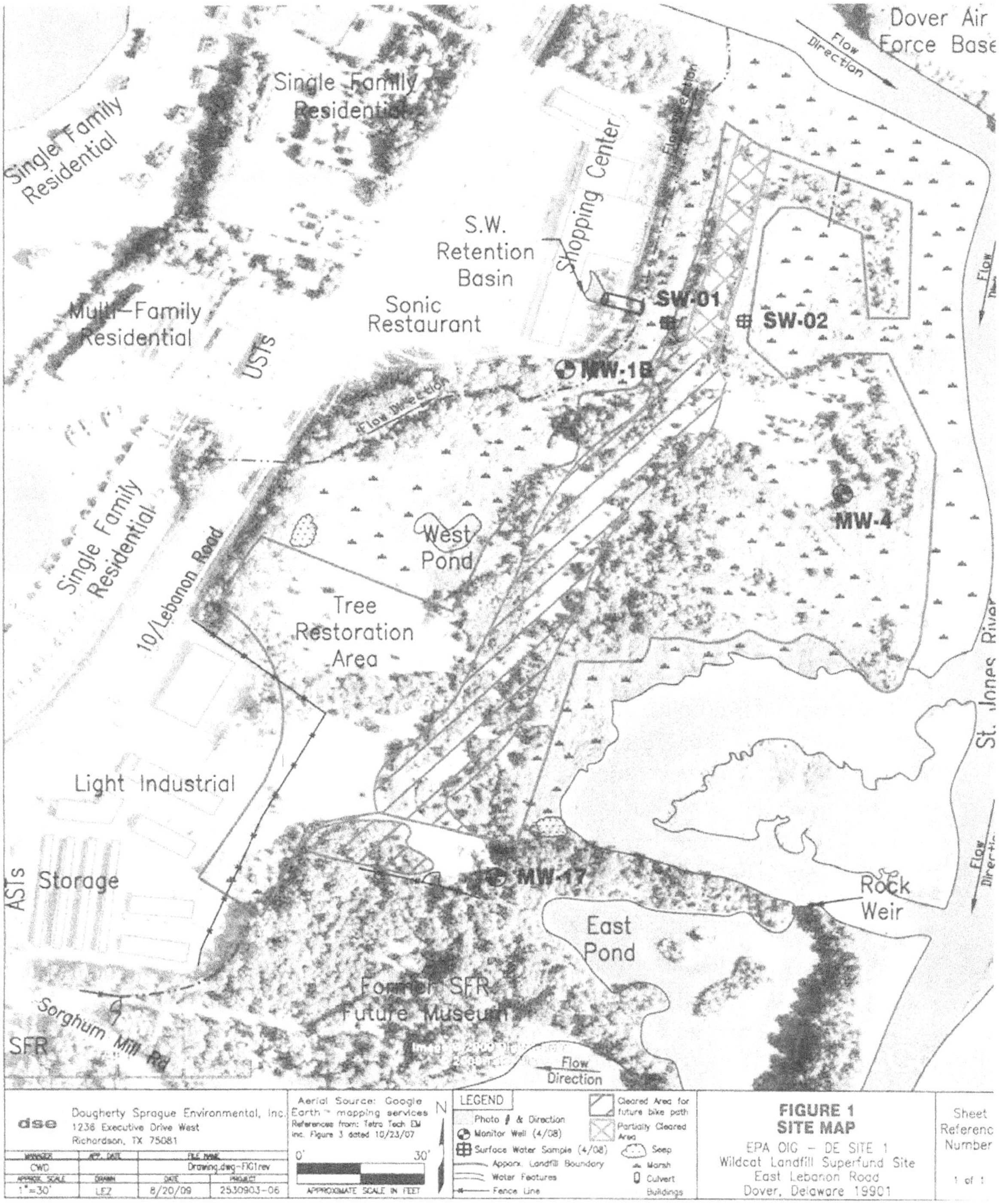

Map Legend

MW – Monitoring wells
SW – Surface water sample locations

----- (Red)	Area for future bike path
----- (Orange)	Light industrial
----- (Pink)	Approximate landfill boundary
----- (Green)	Partially cleared area

Source: EPA OIG contractor.

A limited site inspection was conducted by OIG staff and the contractor. OIG staff members were present during the contractor's inspection and sampling to ensure that proper sampling and site inspection quality assurance protocols were followed. According to the RODs, the primary contaminants of concern affecting the soil and ground water at the Site are volatile organic compounds (VOCs), semi-volatile organic compounds (SVOCs), polychlorinated biphenyls (PCBs), and metals. Therefore, the samples OIG collected were analyzed by qualified laboratories for metals, pesticides, PCBs, VOCs, and SVOCs.

To accomplish our data comparisons, we compared our results to historical data spanning back to 2002. OIG sampling results greater than two standard deviations above the average EPA historical concentrations were considered different. Our review did not include a full evaluation of the reasons for these differences. Where we observed differences, we compared OIG results to the relevant federal and State standards to determine whether OIG's data had implications for human health or environmental protection. The relevant health-based standard is the Delaware Water Quality Criteria for Protection of Aquatic Life.

There were seven compounds for which the OIG's results were higher than Region 3's historical results. For three of those compounds (aluminum, iron, and manganese), our results were biased high and could not be expected to match historical data. For the four remaining compounds (magnesium, potassium, calcium, and sodium), there are no applicable State or federal standards to determine whether these results could have an adverse impact on human health and the environment. Appendix A shows the results of comparing the OIG sample results and the Region's historical data.

We also compared all OIG results to the applicable standard listed in the ROD by comparing our groundwater sampling results to the Delaware DNREC Freshwater Chronic Quality Criteria for Protection of Aquatic Life (DNREC standard). We identified all OIG results that exceeded the DNREC standard.

A draft of this report was sent to the Acting Region 3 Administrator for official comment. Region 3's comments on the draft report are in Appendix C.

Chapter 2
More Sampling and Monitoring of Land Use Changes Needed

Our inspection of the Wildcat Landfill Superfund Site, combined with the land use plans of the Site's owner (Kent County), demonstrate that more sampling and increased EPA oversight of land use changes are needed. The surface waters at the Site have a sheen that resembles petroleum, but the Region has not tested for petroleum in the past and the remedy is not designed to address petroleum contamination. Region 3 agreed with OIG concerns about possible petroleum contamination and tested for it in September 2009. The results showed petroleum was found onsite at levels the Region reported were below the median State action levels, and Region 3 will continue to monitor for petroleum contamination. Kent County plans to use the Site for public recreation that is inconsistent with acceptable uses determined by EPA. Kent County's proposed reuse plans would call for increased Region 3 oversight.

Site Contains Newly Identified Petroleum Products

During our physical inspection of the site we observed a sheen on the surface waters throughout the site. The sheen was iridescent and oily in appearance (see photo below). While this sheen could be harmless, it could also indicate the presence of a petroleum product. Region 3 personnel said they were aware of the sheen at the Site but had concluded that it was naturally occurring.

Iridescent sheen at Wildcat Landfill, April 2008. (EPA OIG photo)

OIG samples from two monitoring wells contained several VOCs, which although found at acceptable levels could also be indicative of the presence of petroleum. Specifically, MW-4 contained benzene, chlorobenzene, chloroethane, ethyl benzene, toluene, and xylenes. MW-17 contained small amounts of benzene and chlorobenzene. These compounds were historically found at the site in concentrations equivalent to OIG results and at levels that do not exceed the DNREC Freshwater Chronic Criteria. In addition, Region 3 reported in its June 2007 Five-Year Review that the amounts of these contaminants present in the historical samples were not in sufficient quantities to indicate a risk to human health and the environment. Appendix B includes all the specific results for the OIG sampling of VOCs.

Waste disposed at the Site could account for the presence of VOCs in samples. Site documents indicate that paint sludge, which contains VOCs, may have been disposed of at the Site. There are also low levels of pesticides, which contain VOCs, historically present in MW-4. This may be the source of the low levels of VOCs in this well. However, VOCs are also indicators of petroleum products. Region 3 considered the possibility of petroleum contamination during its remedial investigation of the Site, but because the VOC levels were so low EPA stated it does not have evidence of petroleum products in subsurface soil, ground water or surface water at levels that indicated petroleum products were a significant concern at the Site. However, analysis of VOCs only is not sufficient for concluding that petroleum products were not a significant concern at the Site. Testing for total petroleum hydrocarbons is also necessary for determining the presence or absence of petroleum.

Because the surface waters at the Site have a sheen and the contaminants consistently found in MW-4 are indicative of petroleum, the presence of gasoline or some other petroleum product at the Site is a possibility. Until September 2009, the Region had not performed a test for petroleum products and, therefore, did not know if petroleum is onsite. Given the landfill's history of violations, Region 3 may not possess complete records of all waste materials disposed in the landfill and may be not be aware of all landfill contaminants. At the request of the OIG, Region 3 sampled the Site for petroleum in September 2009. In December 2009, the Region reported that there is petroleum on the Site at levels below median State action levels. The Region will continue to sample for petroleum to reliably establish the levels of petroleum present onsite and evaluate whether petroleum hydrocarbons are present at levels that would adversely impact human health or the environment.

Metal Concentrations Exceed State Standards

We compared OIG sampling results to the DNREC Freshwater Chronic Quality Criteria for Protection of Aquatic Life to determine whether there were any OIG results that exceed the standard. Of the 197 compounds analyzed, in some cases our results for aluminum, iron, and selenium exceeded the DNREC standard (see Table 2-1). Region 3's historical data for these compounds also exceeded the DNREC Freshwater Chronic Quality Criteria for Protection of Aquatic Life.

Table 2-1: OIG and Region 3 Historical Data that Exceed the Standard

Total Metals (mg/L)	Delaware Freshwater Chronic Standard (DNREC) (mg/L)	Sampling Location	Region 3 Historical Data					OIG Sample Results April 2008 (mg/L)
			May 2002	May 2003	May 2004	August 2006	August 2007	
Aluminum	0.087	MW-17	0.0112 B	< 0.2	0.29	0.59 B	<0.2	0.11
		SW-01	--	--	--	0.877 B	3.97	0.48
		SW-02	--	--	--	10.2	0.74	2.2
Iron	1	MW-1B	0.051 B	<0.2	<0.2	<0.1	<0.1	3.5*
		MW-17	45.5	37	49	65.6	57.8	61.6
		SW-01	--	--	--	25.7	129	69.1
		SW-02	--	--	--	27.8	13.7	96.0
Selenium	0.005	MW-4	0.0038 B	<0.03	<0.03	<0.035	<0.035	0.0129
		MW-17	< 0.002	< 0.03	< 0.03	< 0.035	< 0.035	0.0113
		SW-02	--	--	--	<0.035	<0.035	0.0182

B – This contaminant was found in the blank processed with this sample. The concentration may be biased high.

mg/L – milligrams per liter

* Note: For sample MW-1B, the OIG sample exhibited matrix effect (properties which interfere with accurate analysis). Under that condition, data are not reliable enough for a valid comparison to the federal and State standards. However, the data are useful for comparison with the other wells and in determining that the type of metals sample being taken at the Site is inappropriate. The sampling point SW-02 is in a different location for each data point but was combined to do a whole site perspective.

Source: OIG analysis based on OIG and Region 3 sampling data.

In addition to the exceedances identified above, Region 3 did not take the appropriate type of sample for the metals analysis. The DNREC standard called for dissolved (filtered) metals samples. However, the Region has historically taken total (unfiltered) metals samples. During its September 2009 sampling event, the Region sampled for dissolved metals (filtered), as required by the DNREC sampling criteria. The levels of aluminum and selenium were within ecological protection standards, but iron levels continued to exceed ecological protection standards. In the future, if the contaminants are consistently above the DNREC standard, the Region will determine the extent of the exceedance spatially and whether it is a continuing release. Additional actions by the Region would include targeted investigations to identify site-specific toxicity values for those compounds to determine whether there is an impact to the wildlife and aquatic life on the Site.

We also found that Region 3 was not analyzing other samples at the level of the standard. As a result, there is the possibility that the Site has contamination above the standard, but it has gone undetected and unaddressed by the Region. For example, the standard for aluminum is 0.087 mg/L, but in August 2007 the lab had only determined that there was less than 0.2 mg/L of aluminum onsite. This means there could have been contamination between 0.087 mg/L and 0.2 mg/L that would not be identified by the lab. For its September 2009 sampling, Region 3 corrected this by having the lab analyze down to the level of the standard. The Region has indicated that it is now informally reviewing each data set as it is received for exceedances to the standard, followed by a formal review of all data during the Five-Year Review.

Modifications to Site Remedy Are Necessary Before Land Can Be Used for Recreation

Region 3 had not stayed current on Kent County's Site reuse plans. Kent County's future plans for the Site include converting the property into a recreational greenway by constructing a bike and pedestrian path through it and allowing unrestricted access to that portion of the Site. However, Region 3's Site remedy only supports reuse of the land as a conservation area and greenway with access restricted to authorized personnel. Kent County has already secured funding for aspects of the project, entered into assistance agreements with the State of Delaware, and has placed a conservation easement on the Site. Region 3 stated that it was aware of the County's plans through its continued oversight of Wildcat, but the Region's oversight has been informal and undocumented. Given the advanced stage of the County's plans, the Region needs to increase its oversight through more frequent contact with the County and to provide direction and guidance throughout the County's project to ensure the Site remains safe.

According to EPA documents, the Site contains natural barriers to human access in the form of the St. Jones River, heavily treed borders, and a locked gate at the entrance of the site. According to Region 3, these barriers, along with the stabilization and capping of contaminated soils onsite, removal of drums, and the implementation of institutional controls in the form of deed restrictions, make the Site protective for a conservation area and restrict access of the Site to trained authorized personnel. Since Kent County purchased the Site in January 2005, it has used it as a conservation area. The purpose of the Site's conservation easement is to assure that the property will be retained forever in its natural scenic, open, historic, and forested condition and to prevent any use of the property that will significantly impair or interfere with its conservation value.

Between October 2005 and March 2008, Kent County entered into transportation enhancement agreements with the State of Delaware for design and review of the project (a recreational greenway with a bike and pedestrian path), conducting a feasibility study, and receiving technical assistance. These agreements, and the fact that the County has already secured funding for the feasibility phase of the project, indicate that the County is committed to making the recreational greenway a reality. The County and/or other partner organizations may also restore the manor house on the property for use as a museum.

When Kent County purchased the property, there was debris and exposed landfill waste at the Site. Region 3 stated in the ROD that future direct contact with wastes is a concern should residential or commercial development occur upon the landfill. Since February 2007, Kent County has cleaned up the debris on the open areas of the Site where the bike and pedestrian path would be. According to Region 3's most recent Five-Year review, this level of clean-up is sufficient for the current use of the land and may be sufficient for the future recreational use if access to the Site is limited to the path only. However, exposed landfill debris remains on parts of the Site, which Kent County states it does not have the resources to remove. The debris could pose a hazard to Site users if access to the entire Site is unrestricted. In response to OIG's concerns, the RPM requested an update from Kent County on how it was progressing with cleaning up the debris and addressing other issues about Site reuse plans. The update provided by Kent County showed that the Region was at least 6 months behind what the County had been doing at the Site and the County's latest plans for controlling site access.

EPA needs to conduct routine and documented oversight of the County's plans and activities to determine necessary modifications to the plans, prevent unsafe exposures, and ensure safe uses of the Site if unrestricted access is permitted or likely to occur. Kent County stated that documented correspondence between the County and Region 3 will be extensive during the development of the design plan that would propose changes in land use at Wildcat. The County has also stated that once developed, a draft of the engineered access management proposal will be sent to Region 3 for design guidance and approval.

In addition to Kent County's Site reuse plans, a local small business owner who owns an acre of the Site inquired about building a storage facility on that acre. In conducting oversight of this activity, Region 3 has communicated to this business owner, via e-mail, that it will need to review the owner's construction plans to ensure the integrity of the remedy is maintained. The deed restrictions imposed by Region 3 prevent the business owner from proceeding with plans without further consulting EPA and receiving permission from the State of Delaware. The deed restriction involves ensuring the landfill cap is not damaged. Routine and documented regional oversight will be needed to ensure the cap is not impacted.

Conclusions

Site conditions have changed at the Wildcat Landfill Superfund Site that necessitate new testing and increased EPA oversight. New contaminants have been detected that the Region needs to monitor to determine potential risks. There are plans to have portions of the Site open to unrestricted public access. Under the proposed site reuse scenario, it is unknown whether known or newly discovered contaminants pose unacceptable risks to human health and the environment. A review of Site clean-up actions and existing engineered and institutional controls needs to be done to determine whether they are adequate for the planned reuses of the Site. As a result of OIG oversight, the sampling protocols for the site have been changed to ensure that the data collected are adequate for monitoring the protectiveness of the Site.

Recommendations

We recommend that the Regional Administrator, Region 3:

2-1   Establish a sampling plan for the monitoring wells and surface waters that includes testing for total petroleum hydrocarbons.

2-2   If petroleum is found on the Site above acceptable and appropriate levels, take action to address the contamination and amend existing site documents or generate new site documents, to ensure the Site is protective of human health and the environment for current and planned land uses.

2-3   Formally document oversight of the Site owners' plans and agreements for use of the Site. This includes an evaluation and determination of the impact of construction or vegetation change on the remedy, and what modifications to the remedy and/or ROD will be needed to support unrestricted access to portions of the Site.

2-4   Change the sampling protocol to include dissolved (filtered) metals analysis. Continue to require that the reporting limits for all analyses are at or below the DNREC standard to ensure that all contamination above the standard is detected. Assess the effect of the sampling results on the protectiveness determination of the Site.

EPA Region 3 Response and OIG Evaluation

Region 3 agreed with all four OIG recommendations. We made changes to the report based on Region 3's comments where appropriate. The Region has initiated corrective actions on Recommendations 2-1, 2-2, and 2-4. Specifically, for Recommendations 2-1 and 2-2, beginning with its September 2009 annual sampling event, Region 3 modified its sampling plan for the monitoring wells and surface waters to include testing for petroleum. In response to the Region's draft report comments, we modified Recommendation 2-2 to require action when and if petroleum levels exceed acceptable and appropriate levels. For Recommendation 2-4, beginning with its September 2009 annual sampling event, the Region modified its sampling protocol to require dissolved metals sampling and that the reporting limits for all analyses are at or below the DNREC standard. Region 3 agreed with Recommendation 2-3 and will document in the Site file discussions held with the Site owner regarding future plans and agreements for use of the Site.

We have designated all report recommendations open with agreed-to actions pending. The Region's draft report response contained generally responsive and acceptable corrective actions. However, additional information, such as estimated milestone completion dates, are required in the Region's final response to the report (90-day response). Appendix C provides the full text of the Region's comments and the OIG's evaluation.

Kent County, Delaware, Response and OIG Evaluation

A portion of the draft report was sent to Kent County's representative for the County's review and comment. Kent County cited no inaccuracies in the draft report but requested that we add additional information to the report. Generally, we did not agree to add additional information because these changes had the effect of modifying the meaning or transparency of OIG statements in ways we were unable to support. OIG added information to the report to acknowledge the efforts Kent County has made to clean and improve the Site since it purchased the Wildcat Landfill in 2005. See Appendix D for the full text of the County's response and the OIG's evaluation.

Status of Recommendations and Potential Monetary Benefits

		RECOMMENDATIONS				POTENTIAL MONETARY BENEFITS (in $000s)	
Rec. No.	Page No.	Subject	Status[1]	Action Official	Planned Completion Date	Claimed Amount	Agreed To Amount
2-1	10	Establish a sampling plan for the monitoring wells and surface waters that includes testing for total petroleum hydrocarbons.	O	Region 3 Administrator			
2-2	10	If petroleum is found on the Site above acceptable and appropriate levels, take action to address the contamination and amend existing site documents or generate new site documents, to ensure the Site is protective of human health and the environment for current and planned land uses	O	Region 3 Administrator			
2-3	10	Formally document oversight of the Site owners' plans and agreements for use of the Site. This includes an evaluation and determination of the impact of construction or vegetation change on the remedy, and what modifications to the remedy and/or ROD will be needed to support unrestricted access to portions of the Site.	O	Region 3 Administrator			
2-4	10	Change the sampling protocol to include dissolved (filtered) metals analysis. Continue to require that the reporting limits for all analyses are at or below the DNREC standard to ensure that all contamination above the standard is detected. Assess the effect of the sampling results on the protectiveness determination of the Site.	O	Region 3 Administrator			

[1] O = recommendation is open with agreed-to corrective actions pending
   C = recommendation is closed with all agreed-to actions completed
   U = recommendation is undecided with resolution efforts in progress

Appendix A

OIG Sample Results Compared to Site Historical Data

OIG compared its sample results to Region 3's historical sample results for the Site. OIG sampling results that were greater than two standard deviations above the average EPA historical concentrations were considered different. The table below shows the differences found.

Sampling Location	Total Metals	Historical Sampling Results					OIG Sample Results
		May 2002 mg/L	May 2003 mg/L	May 2004 mg/L	August 2006 mg/L	August 2007 mg/L	April 2008 mg/L
MW-1B	Aluminum	0.0428 B	<0.2	<0.2	0.446 B	<0.2	3.6*
MW-1B	Iron	0.051 B	<0.2	<0.2	<0.1	<0.1	3.5*
MW-1B	Manganese	0.0358 B	<0.05	<0.05	0.0268	0.0307	0.15*
MW-4	Calcium	47	52	56	51.2	64.7	70
MW-4	Magnesium	27.3	28	32	27.8	38.8	44
MW-4	Potassium	62.1	58	67	58.3	66.7	100
MW-4	Sodium	149	140	160	127	231 K	253

B – This contaminant was found in the blank processed with this sample. The concentration may be biased high.
K – Reported value may be biased high. Actual value is expected to be lower.

* For sample MW-1B the OIG sample exhibited matrix effect (properties which interfere with accurate analysis). Under that condition, the result cannot be expected to match the historical data.

Source: OIG analysis based on OIG and Region 3 sampling data.

VOC Results from OIG Sampling

The values in bold in the table below are compounds detected from our sampling. The presence of several of these highlighted contaminants, along with the sheen observed at the Site, indicate that petroleum may be present on the Site.

Compound	MW-1B (µg/L)	MW-17 (µg/L)	MW-4 (µg/L)
Acetone	< 50.0	< 50.0	< 50.0
Benzene	< 1.00	**1.23**	**22.5**
Bromochloromethane	< 1.00	< 1.00	< 1.00
Bromodichloromethane	< 1.00	< 1.00	< 1.00
Bromoform	< 1.00	< 1.00	< 1.00
Bromomethane	< 1.00	< 1.00	< 1.00
2-Butanone	< 50.0	< 50.0	< 50.0
Carbon disulfide	< 1.00	< 1.00	< 1.00
Carbon tetrachloride	< 1.00	< 1.00	< 1.00
Chlorobenzene	< 1.00	**6.80**	**17.7**
Chlorodibromomethane	< 1.00	< 1.00	< 1.00
Chloroethane	< 1.00	< 1.00	**800**
Chloroform	< 1.00	< 1.00	< 1.00
Chloromethane	< 1.00	< 1.00	< 1.00
Cyclohexane	< 5.00	< 5.00	< 5.00
1,2-Dibromo-3-chloropropane	< 5.00	< 5.00	< 5.00
1,2-Dibromoethane (EDB)	< 1.00	< 1.00	< 1.00
Methylcyclohexane	< 5.00	< 5.00	< 5.00
1,2-Dichlorobenzene	< 1.00	< 1.00	**1.42**
1,3-Dichlorobenzene	< 1.00	< 1.00	< 1.00
1,4-Dichlorobenzene	< 1.00	**2.21**	**3.81**
Dichlorodifluoromethane	< 1.00	< 1.00	< 1.00
1,2-Dichloroethane	< 1.00	< 1.00	< 1.00
1,1-Dichloroethane	< 1.00	< 1.00	< 1.00
1,1-Dichloroethene	< 1.00	< 1.00	< 1.00
trans-1,2-Dichloroethene	< 1.00	< 1.00	< 1.00
1,1,2 -Trifluorotrichloroethane	< 1.00	< 1.00	< 1.00
cis-1,2-Dichloroethene	< 1.00	**2.53**	< 1.00
1,2-Dichloropropane	< 1.00	< 1.00	< 1.00
trans-1,3-Dichloropropene	< 1.00	< 1.00	< 1.00
cis-1,3-Dichloropropene	< 1.00	< 1.00	< 1.00
Ethylbenzene	< 1.00	< 1.00	**4.23**
2-Hexanone	< 50.0	< 50.0	< 50.0
Isopropylbenzene	< 1.00	< 1.00	**13.3**
Methyl Acetate	< 10.0	< 10.0	< 10.0
Methyl tert-Butyl Ether	< 1.00	< 1.00	< 1.00
Methylene Chloride	< 5.00	< 5.00	< 5.00

Compound	MW-1B (µg/L)	MW-17 (µg/L)	MW-4 (µg/L)
4-Methyl-2-pentanone	< 10.0	< 10.0	< 10.0
Styrene	< 1.00	< 1.00	< 1.00
1,1,2,2-Tetrachloroethane	< 1.00	< 1.00	< 1.00
Tetrachloroethene	< 1.00	< 1.00	< 1.00
Toluene	< 1.00	< 1.00	**9.35**
1,2,4-Trichlorobenzene	< 1.00	< 1.00	< 1.00
1,2,3-Trichlorobenzene	< 1.00	< 1.00	< 1.00
1,1,1-Trichloroethane	< 1.00	< 1.00	< 1.00
1,1,2-Trichloroethane	< 1.00	< 1.00	< 1.00
Trichloroethene	< 1.00	< 1.00	< 1.00
Trichlorofluoromethane	< 1.00	< 1.00	< 1.00
Vinyl chloride	< 1.00	< 1.00	< 1.00
Xylenes, total	< 3.00	< 3.00	**23.1**

Source: OIG sampling data.

EPA Region 3 Response to Draft Report and OIG Evaluation

UNITED STATES ENVIRONMENTAL PROTECTION AGENCY
REGION III
1650 Arch Street
Philadelphia, Pennsylvania 19103-2029

December 17, 2009

MEMORANDUM

SUBJECT: Response to Draft Evaluation Report: *Changes in Conditions at Wildcat Landfill Superfund Site in Delaware Call for Increased EPA Oversight, Project No. 2008-538, November 3, 2009*

FROM: Shawn M. Garvin, Regional Administrator
Office of the Regional Administrator (3RA00)

TO: Carolyn Copper
Director for Program Evaluation
Hazardous Waste Issues
Office of Inspector General

This is Region III's response to the Office of Inspector General (OIG) draft Evaluation Report: *Changes in Conditions at Wildcat Landfill Superfund Site in Delaware Call for Increased EPA Oversight, dated November 3, 2009.* Overall, Region III agrees with the findings of the report. Outlined below are the Region's responses to the proposed recommendations and a corrective action plan for agreed upon actions, including planned completion dates.

OIG Recommendations for the Wildcat Landfill Superfund Site (Site)

2-1   Establish a sampling plan for the monitoring wells and surface waters that includes testing for total petroleum hydrocarbons.

EPA Corrective Action

Beginning with its September 2009 annual sampling event at the Site, EPA modified its sampling plan for the monitoring wells and surface waters at the Site to include testing for total petroleum hydrocarbons (TPH). A map showing the Site area, and highlighting the Sampling Locations is included as Attachment 1 to this memo.

Summary tables of the results of EPA Region III's September 2009 sampling are included as Attachment 2. EPA will continue to monitor for TPH as long as is necessary to reliably establish the levels of TPH present onsite and evaluate whether petroleum hydrocarbons are present at levels that would adversely impact human health or the environment.

> **OIG Response 1:** Region 3's corrective action for Recommendation 2-1 meets the intent of the recommendation. This recommendation is open with agreed to actions pending. In its 90-day response, the Region should provide milestone dates for the future sampling events where petroleum will be tested.

2-2   If petroleum is found on the Site, determine actions needed to address the contamination and amend existing site documents or generate new site documents, to ensure the Site is protective of human health and the environment for current and planned land uses.

EPA Corrective Action

Total Petroleum Hydrocarbons (or TPH) are a large family of several hundred chemical compounds that come from crude oil. TPH analysis is often used as a screening tool for suspected leaking undergrounds storage tanks. TPH analysis is further broken down into TPH-GRO (gasoline range organics) and TPH-DRO (diesel range organics). There are no federal regulations or action levels specific to TPH. Only 14 states regulate TPH. For the ones that do, the median action level is 1700 ug/L[1].

For the purpose of projecting potential risks associated with exposure to petroleum products, because toxicity varies dramatically among compounds, identifying levels of the individual constituents provides far greater value than reporting the total concentration. In the Superfund Program, the most toxic elements of TPH -- benzene, toluene, ethylbenzene and xylene -- are, in fact, measured during routine analytical services. Then, screening is performed on these compounds to determine if a potential risk exists. (Note that quantifying risks associated with TPH is not possible.) These steps were taken at the Site. Based on the most recent sampling data for the Site (September 2009), of these compounds only benzene was detected at a noteworthy concentration (26 ug/L) in one onsite well (MW-4). However, given the expected future use of the Site (recreational), the observed concentration of benzene in groundwater poses no significant risk under a typical exposure scenario.

For the reasons outlined above, Region III continues to prefer individual compound analysis vs. TPH analysis for risk assessment purposes. At OIG's suggestion the Region is now routinely conducting TPH analysis on samples from the Site. The

---

[1] Moran, Robert. "Health-Based TPH Closure Levels in RISC" Powerpoint Presentation. Indiana Dept. of Environmental Management, October 2009.

results of EPA's September 2009 sampling of monitoring wells and surface water locations at the Site for TPH-GRO and TPH-DRO (See Attachments 1 and 2) showed contaminants present in some samples at relatively low levels. The highest detection (750 ug/L of TPH-DRO in MW-1B), was less than half the median state action level of 1700 ug/L. A few noteworthy facts about the September 2009 TPH sampling results are:

1. MW-1B, the location of the highest detection of TPH-DRO, is a monitoring well located upgradient of the Site, indicating that that contamination is likely not related to the Site. Because it is below action levels, however, further investigation of that result is not warranted.

2. The two surface water samples collected in locations with a visible oily sheen (SW-03 and SW-04) contained the lowest levels of TPH-DRO of any of the surface water samples collected on the Site as part of this sampling event (100 and 70 ug/L, respectively). SW-04 was the only surface water sampling location to have a detection of TPH-GRO, but that value (74 ug/L) was below the Contract-Required Quantitation Limit (CRQL), and therefore "J" qualified (the "J" qualifier means "Analyte present. Reported value may not be accurate or precise.").

3. TPH was detected in one of the blank samples leading all the TPH results to be "B" qualified, meaning the contaminant was "not detected at levels substantially above the level reported in laboratory or field blanks." Blank contamination indicates the sample results may be biased high, but because the reported results are still below action levels these results are still usable.

➤ **OIG Response 2:** Region 3 generally agreed with Recommendation 2-2. In response to the Region's draft report comments, we modified Recommendation 2-2 to require action when and if petroleum levels exceed acceptable and appropriate levels. According to the Region's draft report comments, its September 2009 sampling showed the highest level of TPH was 750 µg/L of TPH. The Region stated that this is less than half the median State action level of 1700 µg/L. However, the Region acknowledges in its comments that monitoring and evaluating individual components of TPH, such as VOCs, is how a risk determination is made. As a result, in addition to conducting TPH testing, the Region will also continue to test for the individual components of TPH. Region 3's corrective action for Recommendation 2-2 meets the intent of the recommendation. This recommendation is open with agreed to actions pending. In its 90-day response to OIG's final report, the Region should describe its planned corrective actions for monitoring levels of TPH, assessing potential risk associated with levels of TPH that exceed acceptable and appropriate levels, and additional actions that should occur to address identified risks, particularly considering Site reuse plans.

2-3   Formally document oversight of the Site owners' plans and agreements for use of the Site. This includes an evaluation and determination of the impact of construction or vegetation change on the remedy, and what modifications to the remedy and/or ROD will be needed to support unrestricted access to portions of the Site.

EPA Corrective Action

To date, the owner's plans for the Site have been quite preliminary and physical realization of those plans has been estimated by the Site owner to be several years off in the future. As it awaits the owner's actions, EPA will document discussions held with the Site owner regarding future plans and agreements for use of the Site in the Site file. Upon receipt of a formal design plan from the Site owner, EPA will complete an evaluation and determine the impact of construction or vegetation change on the remedy, and what modifications to the remedy and/or ROD will be needed to support any changes to access to portions of the Site that may be part of such a design.

> **OIG Response 3**: Region 3's corrective action for Recommendation 2-3 meets the intent of the recommendation. This recommendation is open with agreed to actions pending. In its 90-day response to OIG's final report, the Region should provide milestone dates for discussions it will initiate and schedule with the Site owner(s) as part of its plan for conducting improved oversight of the Site reuse plans.

2-4   Change the sampling protocol to include dissolved (filtered) metals analysis. Require that the reporting limits for all analyses are at or below the DNREC standard to ensure that all contamination above the standard is detected. Assess the effect of the sampling results on the protectiveness determination of the Site.

EPA Corrective Action

Beginning with its September 2009 annual sampling event at the Site, EPA modified its sampling plan for the monitoring wells and surface waters at the Site to require that the reporting limits for all analyses are at or below the DNREC standard to ensure that all contamination above the standard is detected. EPA will carry this practice forward in all future sampling events at the Site. EPA will assess the effect of the sampling results on the protectiveness determination of the Site informally upon receipt of each set of validated sampling data, and formally no less frequently than once every five years as part of its Five Year Review. The next Five Year Review for the Site is scheduled to be completed in July 2012.

> **OIG Response 4:** Region 3's corrective action for Recommendation 2-4 meets the intent of the recommendation and milestones have been provided.

Attachment 1 – Sampling Location Map (labeled "Figure 3")
Attachment 2 – Summary Tables of Analytical Results for Organic (labeled "Appendix C") and
        Inorganic Compounds (labeled "Appendix D") Detected in Groundwater and Surface
        Water Samples collected at Wildcat Landfill Superfund Site, September 2009.

OIG Note: The OIG did not include the attachments in this report.

Appendix D

Kent County Response to Draft Report and OIG Evaluation

Denis K. Mumford
Director - Acting
Community Services
(302) 744-2486
(302) 760-4757 Fax

Hillary Welliver
Assistant Director
Community Services
Division of Library Services
(302) 698-6444
(302) 760-4757 Fax

Kent **County**

Department of Community Services

Jeremy Sheppard
Assistant Director - Acting
Community Services
Divisions of
Parks & Recreation
(302) 744-2494
(302) 760-4757 Fax

Carl J. Solberg
Projects & Grants
Administrator
Parks Division
(302) 744-2490
(302) 760-4757

D. Denise Rice
1200 Pennsylvania NW
MC2460T
Washington, D.C. 20460

December 22, 2009

Dear Ms. Rice,

Please may this serve to provide the comments of the Kent County Parks Division regarding the EPA OIG's 11/03/09 Draft Summary and Recommendations from OIG's 2009 site review of the Wildcat Landfill. Thank you for the opportunity. This correspondence replaces our email of November 30, 2009 in which this information was provided by addendum to the Adobe Acrobat file provided by EPA for the County's response.

Also, permit us to thank EPA for its diligence to monitor the effectiveness of the institutional controls at the Wildcat Landfill. Kent County is indebted to the rigorous attention your office and Region III have given to this project. The County's work and public service at Wildcat are both supported and enhanced by EPA's endeavors.

As you know from earlier correspondence, (ref. 07/22/09 email to Patrick Milligan) Kent County Parks has engaged in many aspects of conservation restoration, cultural resources preservation, voluntary enhanced remediation of landfill areas where EPA found site controls to be unnecessary, proactive restriction of access conditions left by EPA, public outreach and community engagement, and considerable grant development. Considerable County revenues and in-kind forces have been deployed to secure, stabilize, and otherwise improve the Wildcat Landfill and its environs.

We are now developing a scope of work for design services by Whitman, Requardt & Associates, P.E., to be procured under a Transportation Enhancement Program grant by DelDOT. This professional services agreement will produce construction plans and other engineering documents together with approvals (including those of Region III) for a bike/ped pathway utilizing the existing geotec & stone road at the Wildcat Landfill. This PS&E scope of work will be based on the earlier concept plan (ref 5/2009 WR&A preliminary conceptual alignment study previously provided to Region III) and will be performed through to completion sometime in calendar 2010.

Kent County is fulfilling its stated intentions, established with Region III at the time of property acquisition in 2004, to enhance the institutional controls established by EPA, elevate the environmental, conservation, cultural preservation, and passive recreational values and uses of the entire property acquired from Shirley L. Hunn. We have maintained continuous, informal correspondence with Region III's Remediation Section and occasionally with our colleagues at DNREC SIRB prior to property acquisition and throughout the County's voluntary additional remediation, and conservation and passive recreation planning which commenced in 2005.

Kent County was inspired by numerous case studies provided by EPA, of beneficial re-use of CERCLA and Brownfields properties for our St. Jones Greenway, and we intend that in the fullness of time this site will provide a correspondingly noteworthy case study for EPA and others. The next phase of site development will complete the conversion of Kent County's additional earthen cap restoration and the landfill cells remediated by EPA to a long-term meadow habitat based on recommendations of the Delaware Wildlife Action Plan and further informed by the County's recognition that scrub shrub woodland conditions can not be supported by the shallow landfill cap.

We find in general, that OIG's summary correctly reflects the overall conditions and planning context for the Wildcat Landfill. It does, however, contain some inaccurate representations of fact and process which these comments are intended to clarify. The conclusion regarding enhancement of the correspondence between Kent County and Region III flows, at least in part, from the impression that OIG has formed that Region III is "….at least 6 months behind what the County had been doing at the Site and the County's latest plans for controlling site access." (Ref. Draft – For Review and Comment Purposes Only, Page 2). We hope the net effect of our response will serve to convince the OIG to amend this impression. We are, in any event, very grateful to Region III for its assistance and will continue to apprize it of all our planning activities as they continue.

The following comments apply to OIG's Draft Summary Report of 11/03/09 and are referenced by numerical notations where they have been inserted in the Word document as applicable. We request that the final report reflect the information provided herein.

1
Kent County prefers the following text:
"...limited pedestrian and bicycle access on a pre-existing stone roadway within the landfill."

#2
Kent County prefers the following text:
"...and placed an earthen cap within non-remediated landfill in all areas adjacent to the intended pathway, leaving distant and environmentally sensitive landfill areas undisturbed due to cost and designation of these areas for non-access."

#3
Kent County disagrees with this characterization as we are developing a design plan to be submitted to EPA for its review..... We prefer the following text:
"...allowing limited bicycle and pedestrian only access on the existing stone roadway and conversion of the landfill cap to a conservation meadow management unit."

#4
Omitted statement of fact,
"....and further restricted unmanaged public access by removing four wooden bridges through the property's forested buffer and installing an additional 500 LF of denial of access fencing where no controls existed."

#5
It is not clear from this sentence that OIG is referring to the voluntary Conservation Easement placed on the property by Kent County and the State of Delaware and recorded at the time of property acquisition in January, 2004.

#6
Omitted information.
"Kent County's contract for professional design services is being developed with DelDOT at this time and will include extensive correspondence requirements with EPA Region III regarding the design plans for this pathway."

#7
Omitted statement of fact,
"In consultation with Region III since 2006, Kent County removed large quantities of surficial domestic waste and trash, and placed an earthen cap over a 12-acre area including all un-remediated landfill areas adjacent to and substantially beyond the existing landfill roadway where the bike and pedestrian path would be."

#8
Clarification is needed.
"....remain on remote parts of the site which are environmentally sensitive and distant from the proposed use of the roadway. These areas are designated for non-disturbance under the conservation management objectives for the Site and access will not be enabled by the County's bike path."

#9
A factual error can be corrected as follows:
"Kent County has not yet engineered its access management proposal as this is a deliverable from its design consultant, and this will be conveyed in draft to Region III for design guidance and approval when it is developed."

#10
"Kent County agrees that documented correspondence between the County and Region III is a requirement of any design plan for passive access to the Conservation Area and Landfill."

#11
"Unrestricted" landfill access is not intended. Kent County has placed more restrictions on access than those left by EPA's remedy - when footpaths and wooden bridges were removed by Kent County and additional fencing was installed in 2006. The proposed bike path on an existing stone roadway will continue to preclude vehicular access. Since the draft concept design plan by WR&A (5/2009) was conveyed to Region III, Kent County has removed the one segment originally envisioned to be placed on landfill cap as not feasible. Approvals of the final selected design plan by Region III will be a deliverable in the actual engineering phase for 2010. Kent County prefers to refer to bike/ped use of the stone roadway as "...managed access to portions of the Site."

Please let me know if I can help you with this or if any additional clarification would be helpful. With EPA's assistance, the Wildcat Landfill will emerge as a persuasive case study of local and federal coordination and community service.

Sincerely,

Carl J. Solberg

Carl J. Solberg
Kent County Parks Division Projects & Grants Administrator

CC: Michael PetitDeMange, Kent County Administrator
        Keith Mumford, Kent County Community Services Director
        Jeremy Sheppard, Kent County Parks and Recreation Director
        Hillary Thornton, Region III Remediation Project Manager
        Patrick J. Milligan, EPA OIG Project Manager

Changes in Conditions at Wildcat Landfill Superfund Site in Delaware Call for Increased EPA Oversight

(**OIG Note:** Kent County's 11 comments to our draft report are inserted in numerical order in the following text.)

At a Glance

The Site's owner has plans to use the Site as a greenway and to construct a bike path on the landfill, which would open part of the Site to unrestricted access.

(Comment 1. Replace "unrestricted" with "...limited pedestrian and bicycle access on a pre-existing stone roadway within the landfill.")

➢ **OIG Response 1:** Based on information available to OIG, the phrase is accurate, transparent, and readable. No changes made.

The owner has cleaned up landfill debris where the bike path would be but indicated it does not have the resources to clean up exposed debris on other parts of the Site.

(Comment 2. Kent County prefers greater clarity as follows: "The Owner has removed landfill debris and placed an earthen cap within non-remediated landfill in all areas adjacent to the intended pathway, leaving distant and environmentally sensitive landfill areas undisturbed due to cost and designation of these areas for non-access.")

➢ **OIG Response 2:** The OIG acknowledges the efforts Kent County has made to further clean and improve the site. These efforts are acknowledged in the *Noteworthy Achievements* section of this report.

In addition, a local small business owner who purchased an acre of the Site has inquired about building a storage facility on that acre. Region 3 is aware of the site-use plans but needs to increase its oversight to ensure unacceptable short- and long-term risks to humans and the environment remain controlled.

Modifications to Site Remedy Are Necessary Before Land Can Be Used for Recreation

Region 3 may not always be current with details of Kent County's reuse plans. Kent County's future plans for the Site include converting the property into a recreational greenway by constructing a bike and pedestrian path through it and allowing unrestricted access to that portion of the Site.

(Comment 3. Kent County disagrees with this characterization as we are developing a design plan to be submitted to EPA for its review..... We prefer the following text: "...and allowing limited bicycle- and pedestrian- only access on the existing stone roadway and conversion of the landfill cap to a conservation meadow management unit.")

➤ **OIG Response 3:** Based on information available to OIG, the phrase is accurate, transparent, and readable. No changes made.

However, Region 3's Site remedy only supports reuse of the land as a conservation area and greenway with access restricted to authorized personnel. Kent County has already secured funding for aspects of the project, entered into assistance agreements with the State of Delaware, and has placed a conservation easement on the Site. Region 3 stated that it was aware of the County's plans through its continued oversight of Wildcat, but the Region's oversight has been informal and undocumented. Given the advanced stage of the County's plans, the Region needs to increase its oversight through more frequent contact with the County and to provide direction and guidance throughout the County's project to ensure the Site remains safe.

According to EPA documents, the Site contains natural barriers to human access in the form of the St. Jones River, heavily treed borders, and a locked gate at the entrance of the site. According to Region 3, these barriers, along with the stabilization and capping of contaminated soils on site, removal of drums, and the implementation of institutional controls in the form of deed restrictions, make the Site protective for a conservation area and restricts access of the Site to trained authorized personnel. Since Kent County purchased the Site in January 2005, it has used it as a conservation area.

(Comment 4. Insert requested. "…and further restricted previously unmanaged public access by removing four wooden bridges through the property's forested buffer and installing an additional 500 LF of denial of access fencing where no controls previously existed.")

➤ **OIG Response 4:** The suggested wording does not add necessary information to the report and the content is not germane to the issue. No changes made.

The purpose of the Site's conservation easement is to assure that the property will be retained forever in its natural scenic, open, historic, and forested condition and to prevent any use of the property that will significantly impair or interfere with its conservation value.

(Comment 5. It is not clear from this sentence that OIG is referring to the voluntary Conservation Easement placed on the property by Kent County and the State of Delaware and recorded at the time of property acquisition in January, 2004.)

➢ **OIG Response 5:** This level of detail is not necessary in the report. No changes made.

Between October 2005 and March 2008, Kent County entered into transportation enhancement agreements with the State of Delaware for design and review of the project (a recreational greenway with a bike and pedestrian path), conducting a feasibility study, and receiving technical assistance. These agreements, and the fact that the County has already secured funding for the feasibility phase of the project, indicate that the County is committed to making the recreational greenway a reality.

(Comment 6. This would be the appropriate place to include: "Kent County's contract for professional design services is being developed with DelDOT at this time and will include extensive correspondence requirements with EPA Region III regarding the design plans for this pathway.")

➢ **OIG Response 6:** The point of this report passage is to substantiate that Kent County is firm in its plans. The additional comments are not needed to further substantiate this for purposes of our report. No changes made.

The County and/or other partner organizations may also restore the manor house on the property for use as a museum.

When Kent County purchased the property, there was debris and exposed landfill waste at the Site. Region 3 stated in the ROD that future direct contact with wastes is a concern should residential or commercial development occur upon the landfill. Since February 2007, Kent County has cleaned up the debris on the open areas of the Site where the bike and pedestrian path would be.

(Comment 7. Insert requested.
"In consultation with Region III since 2005, Kent County removed large quantities of surficial domestic waste and trash, and placed an earthen cap over a 12-acre area including all un-remediated landfill areas adjacent to and substantially beyond the existing landfill roadway where the bike and pedestrian path would be.")

➢ **OIG Response 7:** The OIG acknowledges the efforts Kent County has made to further clean and improve the site. These efforts are acknowledged in the *Noteworthy Achievements* section of this report.

According to Region 3's most recent Five-Year review, this level of clean-up is sufficient for the current use of the land and may be sufficient for the future recreational use if access to the Site is limited to the path only. However, exposed landfill debris remains on parts of the Site, which Kent County states it does not have the resources to remove.

(Comment 8. Insert requested. "However, exposed landfill debris remains on remote parts of the site which are environmentally sensitive and distant from the proposed use of the roadway. These areas are designated for non-disturbance under the conservation management objectives for the Site and access will not be enabled by the County's bike path.")

➢ **OIG Response 8:** In Kent County's e-mail of October 28, 2008, it stated the following, "The minor examples of incidental trash exposed by throw-down which they observed, are in the margins of the uncapped landfill that our resources can not reach." The language the OIG uses in the report is an accurate portrayal of what the OIG observed and the County's response to the condition at the site.

The debris could pose a hazard to Site users if access to the entire Site is unrestricted. In response to OIG's concerns, the RPM requested an update from Kent County on how it was progressing with cleaning up the debris and addressing other issues about site reuse plans. The update provided by Kent County showed that the Region was at least 6 months behind what the County had been doing at the Site and the County's latest plans for controlling site access.

(Comment 9. Insert requested. "Kent County has not yet engineered its access management proposal as this is a deliverable from its design consultant, and this will be conveyed in draft to Region III for design guidance and approval when it is developed. Also, the May 2009 Conceptual Plan for use of the existing roadway as a bike path was previously transmitted to Region III.")

➢ **OIG Response 9:** The OIG understands that the County's plans are still being formulated. However, this portion of the report is referring to the situation as it existed during the early part of the OIG's evaluation, before May 2009. Region 3 stated that it was aware of the County's plans through its continued oversight of Wildcat, but the Region's oversight has been informal and undocumented.

EPA needs to conduct routine and documented oversight of the County's plans and activities to determine necessary modifications to the plans, prevent unsafe exposures, and ensure safe uses of the Site if unrestricted access is permitted or likely to occur.

(Comment 10. Insert requested. "Kent County agrees that documented correspondence between the County and Region III is a requirement of any design plan for passive access to the Conservation Area and Landfill.")

➤ **OIG Response 10:** The OIG agrees and will revise the report accordingly.

Recommendation

Formally document oversight of the Site owners' plans and agreements for use of the Site. This includes an evaluation and determination of the impact of construction or vegetation change on the remedy, and what modifications to the remedy and/or ROD will be needed to support unrestricted access to portions of the Site.

(Comment 11. "Unrestricted" landfill access is not intended. Kent County has placed more restrictions on access than those left by EPA's remedy - when footpaths and wooden bridges were removed by Kent County and additional fencing was installed in 2006. The proposed bike path on an existing stone roadway will continue to preclude vehicular access. Since the draft concept design plan by WR&A (5/2009) was conveyed to Region III, Kent County has removed the one segment originally envisioned to be placed on landfill cap as not feasible. Approvals of the final selected design plan by Region III will be a deliverable in the actual engineering phase for 2010. Kent County prefers to refer to bike/ped use of the stone roadway as "...managed access to portions of the Site.")

➤ **OIG Response 11:** The OIG report modifies the term unrestricted by using it in conjunction with the phrase, "on portions of the Site." The OIG understands that the County and EPA Region 3 plan additional restrictions to keep the public on the intended path. However, until the access management plans are complete and available for evaluation, it cannot be determined if the controls are a sufficient deterrent to accessing parts of the Site that are not intended for public use.

Distribution

Office of the Administrator
Assistant Administrator, Office of Solid Waste and Emergency Response
Regional Administrator, Region 3
Principal Deputy Assistant Administrator, Office of Solid Waste and Emergency Response
Director, Office of Superfund Remediation and Technology Innovation, Office of Solid Waste
      and Emergency Response
Agency Follow-up Official (the CFO)
Agency Follow-up Coordinator
General Counsel
Associate Administrator for Congressional and Intergovernmental Relations
Associate Administrator for Public Affairs
Audit Follow-up Coordinator, Office of Solid Waste and Emergency Response
Audit Follow-up Coordinator, Region 3
Acting Inspector General